Pocahontas
The Life of an Indian Princess

Colleen Adams

Rosen Classroom Books & Materials
New York

Published in 2003 by The Rosen Publishing Group, Inc.
29 East 21st Street, New York, NY 10010

Copyright © 2003 by The Rosen Publishing Group, Inc.

Book Design: Ron A. Churley

Photo Credits: Cover, pp. 1, 7, 8 © Hulton/Archive; pp. 4, 10–11, 12, 14 © Bettman/Corbis.

ISBN: 0-8239-6385-3
6-pack ISBN: 0-8239-9567-4

Manufactured in the United States of America

Contents

Pocahontas and the Powhatans

Pocahontas (poh-kuh-HAHN-tuhs) was an Indian princess. She lived with her father, Chief Powhatan, the leader of the Powhatan Indians. The Powhatans lived in what is now the eastern part of Virginia. Pocahontas was about twelve years old in 1607 when some English **colonists** arrived. The colonists formed the first English **colony** in America. They named this colony Jamestown.

> Pocahontas was an active and happy young woman. "Pocahontas" means "playful one."

Helping Neighbors

Pocahontas wanted to know more about the colonists and visited them often. She saw that the colonists did not have much food, so she brought them corn and fish. She learned to speak English so she could talk to them. Pocahontas became friends with one of the leaders of the colony, Captain John Smith.

Pocahontas traded food and furs to the colonists for toys and tools that she took back to the Powhatans.

Pocahontas and John Smith

There are many stories about Pocahontas and her friendship with Captain John Smith. Captain Smith wrote a story about being **captured** by the Powhatan Indians. He wrote that the Powhatans would have killed him if Pocahontas had not stopped them. Today, many people do not believe this story is true.

Captain Smith wrote that Pocahontas ran to his side and begged her father to save his life.

Taken by the Colonists

The Powhatans and the colonists had many **disagreements**. Some of the colonists made a plan to trick Pocahontas. They took her away from her home, hoping that Chief Powhatan would give them food and land to get his daughter back. The chief gave the colonists some of the things they wanted, but the colonists did not send Pocahontas home.

More colonists continued to arrive at Jamestown. The English colonists taught Pocahontas their way of life in the colony.

John Rolfe

Pocahontas lived with the colonists for many years. She learned how to dress and speak like the colonial women. The colonists gave her the name Rebecca. Pocahontas met and fell in love with John Rolfe, an English colonist. They were married in 1614. The next year, Pocahontas and John had a son named Thomas.

After Pocahontas and John Rolfe were married, the Powhatans and colonists lived together peacefully for many years.

13

Pocahontas Travels to England

In 1616, the Rolfe family went to England. Many people wanted to meet Pocahontas. A famous artist painted her picture. The king and queen of England had parties for her. On the ship back to Virginia, Pocahontas became very sick and died. She will always be remembered for helping the colonists and the Powhatans live together in peace.

Glossary

capture   To take someone by force against their will.

colonist   Someone who moves to a new land but stays under the rule of their old country.

colony   Land that has been settled by people who live in one country but are ruled by another country.

disagreement   When people have different ideas about something.

Index